Beautiful Encounter...

Joanna Kantharia

BookLeaf
Publishing

India | USA | UK

Presentation by *BookLeaf Publishing*

Web: www.bookleafpub.com

E-mail: info@bookleafpub.com

ISBN: 9789363319332

First edition 2024

to papa...

PREFACE

Joanna, an old-schoolish old soul. A yet unpublished anthology by herself and in herself. She, an unbridled, gurgling brook, has gathered her experiences, as she unabashedly and mindfully flows along in her journey, nonchalantly brushing aside any and every impediment. An accomplished professional with an enviable body of work in Business Ethics, Corporate governance, and Risk Mitigation. Joanna pours her soul into her poems, which is why each of these is as unique as they come. Tempestuous yet serene, fire and brimstone yet snow flaky, in your face yet standoffish, she remains undefiable, unless reduced to the narrow, hyphenated polarities of her persona, which, in essence, will not ever be enough to define who she is! Her poems are what she is; alive, rapturous, effervescent, deep, redolent of love, loss, heartache, and unbridled passion. Therefore, enjoy her offerings. Even if you can't completely understand them, I'm sure they'll touch you just where you can feel, feel the heady rush of a cocktail of emotion. That's Joanna, a cocktail; discovered yet unexplored and unnamed. Sink your heart and soul and enjoy a dreamy, unfettered flight!

Inherent Pathos...

Do you feel...
It's tough to say goodbyes...
It's hard to let a teardrop fall by…
It's strange how you let love enmesh your being...
When you really never had a thing going therein...

Do you feel...
I was the one who held your heart...
I was the one who changed your path...
I was the one who whirled your world...
I never meant to challenge your thoughts...

Do you feel...
Life would be easy if you hadn't met me...
The need to say that you never loved me...
Never want to hold me tight at night...
Tell me this only when, in my grave, I lie...

Desire

Come come my love with the wings of a bird
I wait for you, but you don't come
I wander for you, but you don't know
Your smiles are enduring, the world seems pleased
Your laughter is intoxicating, the world rejoices
Come come my love with the wings of a bird
I'll hold you in my arms and never let you down…

You are my dream, you are my passion
You are the one who makes me shine
You are the love molded for me
You are the statue of my life
Come come my love with the wings of a bird
And hold me in your arms and never let me down...

Blinded By Love

3

Intense love is blind, heard people say
Blinded for life, I follow thee everywhere
Never seem to hunger or feel the ache
Tripping and falling, I still walk your way...

Dreamt I, one lonely night, and petrified I grew
You are holding someone else, and the closeness
brewed
Scurried away my thoughts and said they were untrue
Believing I slept, not only did I love you, but so did
you

Dawned the morning with fullness of promises
Little did I know, the day ahead was very stormy
Hardly could I bear the thought of seeing you leave
But follow thee even today, 'cause am blinded
anyways...

An Affair With a Star

This one STAR fondly stares at me
Each night as darkness befalls me
Gives me company for many hours
Though, cannot reach me from distance so far

This one STAR is a joy to gaze
Brightly shining all by itself
Tells me the story of a guy like him
Stood tall among all his fellow beings

This one STAR I wonder if it's sad
Yearning for love in eternal space
The man I love is just like him
Vibrant and lively but all so lonely

Hey you, STAR, I do adore you
If I could, I would come with you
But for all I can, I will always do
Share precious moments in life with you...

Gratification; Every Inch…

For a drop of love, I do thank thee
Extended when I am not a part of thee
Stolen moments, I'll forever cherish these
Missing you when I am not around thee...

Apparent is my being sheltered scarcely
Shivering under your spell dying gladly
Surfaced your love so clear, thy can't bury
Fate playing games lost we are and cannot scurry

Gently hold; don't let the bloom pass by ever
Tactless words will leave a scar and go never
There is a world filled with love of ageless genres
Grab the one that you hold closest, my dear

Wish for the rains of passion to come once more
Drench me subtly with ardent love and adore
Promises I have none and pain much more
Will you come, love? I'll be waiting for
evermore...

Distant Love

Aren't your eyes painfully mourn?
Taking my peace, depart the groan;
Sprinkle your love, bless me, I pray,
I do need you, come what may.

Aren't your arms searching me?
Reach my soul and unfold your wings;
I do wonder why the space,
Isn't the shore blessed with waves?

Aren't there desires underneath your heart?
There are my tears, like dewdrops fall;
Give me a word to let me know,
Am I there locked in your thoughts?

Aren't you staying from love so far?
Please don't sulk when the days are past.
All I know and all I care is,
That distant love will tear my life apart.

Sunshine

Ask me not if I have gains in my life
Whether I want to win or lose the race of life
For all I know, my life is full of pleasure
'Cause you have bought the sunshine in my life

Your love has eased the pain away
Grateful I am, forever to thee, so stay
Delight, I show fears though none
But glad I am for the sunshine in my life

Who would know better than you;
My cravings for love that I never did show
My heart skips a beat at every thought of you,
Thanks for being the sunshine in my life

Faith and trust I have met in you,
Incessantly, my love, I'll believe in you
Near or far, I'll count my blessings with you.
You'll be forever,
remember;

Remain the Sunshine in my
life...

Whispering Love

Whispers of love are a great delight
Tell me a dozen, and I still may shy
Frozen with love my heartbeats struggle
Closeness makes my senses shuffle

Pierces through me your loving stare
Wish me that I stand and let love sway
Gently touch the fears away
Show me a way to live and bear

Harrow in me your love divine
I'll follow my dreams till the day I lie
Absence of love piles tears in my life
Distance will kill me; I promise I'll die...

Twin Flame

The Sparks were all around the first time we met
Who knows what caused you to be my soulmate
The intense sense of attraction, recognition, and
longing
The familiar and undeniable bond felt like
homecoming

My soul found a companion, and you felt the
connection
Nothing short of a miracle, destiny devised such a
union
Our eyes met, the souls danced to a beautiful song of
gold
Melted hearts rummaged through the memoir of lives
from ages old

You are my Twin Flame in all the universes and lives
Following one after the other from spaces far and
wide
Elated my being for bonding and reuniting despite all
defies
Bringing a healing touch to each other on this earth
sublime

Wedded in the spiritual realms ever since we were
created
The nuptials on earth are merely a formality by men,
twisted
Never to part in any form from thee, in this life or
next
Forever I remain conjugated with thee... yours truly,
Twin Flame

Phenomenal Destiny!

Sentenced my love will be if I ever reveal
Locked in my heart it is, so vulnerable that is
Search my being and you'll find a hurting split
Oozing with love, coz it's difficult to seize...

Many a juncture I find questions and stares
Many faces that tell my love was nothing but a snare
You ignored or avoided can't really share
Did the same faces surround you and give you a
scare?

Restored my faith was in time and tide to come
Reveling in life, my years freely flowed along.
Destined were we to subsist and forego all the sorrow
Brushed away, the memories went in a lane furrow...

Erupts my emotions at your slightest sight today
Thought they were murdered and lay in vain away
Thumping of my heart does not cease to be
You came running and calling as a friend in need be

Intricate becomes my life and sorry my state
If only I revealed my love on that very day
How do I tell my present about my past decay?
Please justify the measures that I take this day...

Fears Unknown

Muster of thoughts crawls my mind
Leave me and go, with Thy love divine
Safe is your heart, unhurt and pure
Encircling my life are Fears Unknown

Autumn of life is all I have
Dreams of sorrow are what I share
Waves of oceans are my being
Withered desires form the strings of me

I pray, for you deserve a life of love
Precious and playful smiles for evermore
True as you, may the love surround...
Holding and cherished without the Fears
unknown...

Adieu

Adieu, my love, strange it may sound
You are not mine, and I can't prove it wrong

Mesmerized your way, my heartbeat flows
Gently caressing my lips, the wind doth flows

Take away this feeling. I beg and plead
Holding my heart every step I breathe

Butterflies in my stomach don't stop fluttering
My moistened eyes don't stop searching

Forever leave and get involved with your strive
Am only a dream; wake up, and forever I'll die

Adieu, my love, strange it may sound
You are not mine, and none can prove it wrong...

Imagery Of Nostalgia

Ardent Dreams are flying around
Watching me play, silence surrounds
Holding them with eyebrows high
Wishing them a lifelong smile

Love passed by giving a naughty smirk
Insolent behavior scattered over the earth
Fair isn't a word that describes the trial
Saddened, my heart follows thy flights

Years have passed and I still hang around
Forgotten like a dewdrop that the morning
brought
Remember I; all your passions so visibly
Like the hues of the season, gently erasing

Gestures hold; don't pound on me
He took my dreams while I was asleep
Call him and ask him where he veiled them
My playful mates, I so very much miss them...

Missing You!

Loneliness stood in my pathway like a lump of
salt
Soreness stared and glared with piercing thorns
all around

Clouds kissed the mountains, and the story
began
Rivers wept and swayed, carrying the moss
around

This is how I miss you when I miss you
Everything seems to go wrong, and I still miss
you

Chirping birds go silent as if a storm in the
sideway
Thousand miles away are you, from where I stay

Hills and valleys grow misty like denied of
sunlight
Highways are empty and far from any common
sight

This is how I miss you when I miss you
Everything seems to go wrong, and I still miss
you

Miss you, baby; it's not me, but my heart always
says
Why is nature behaving so strangely all these
days?

My body and soul travel a different course
altogether
Soul in search of thee every single night or day,
no matter

This is how I miss you when I miss you
Everything seems to go wrong, and I still miss
you...

What You Mean To Me! ! !

Life brings us to such turns
When we just cannot say
Why do we find so much joy
In a certain thought or way
Why does a kiss matter
So very very much?
Why do we thrill so deeply
Why does your look or smile
Mean so very much to me?
And your arms around my shoulders
Bring such a wealth of ecstasy?
Forgive me, dear one
For this feeling of mine
For the warmth of your lips
Is as heady as wine
Forgive me for craving
The look in your eyes
And the touch of your fingers
Which wipes out all the 'Whys'

All But LOVE!

In all fairness, I will, and I will for sure
Tell you my story, my story of Love

Stone of Heart or Heart of Stone hath he
Beneath that sweet smile, a smile of goldy

Friend, he called me, called me many names
But he never heard, heard my cry of pain

Words he gave and words had no meaning
Will he acknowledge my being, was a distant
dream

Shattered I lie and lie with my shattered heart
Nostalgia of days, the days those are gone past

Left the scars, many scars of emotional turmoil
Took away my peace, the peace for a lifetime

Among the things he gave, gave passions of
desires

The only thing he did not give, he did not give
LOVE! ! !

Aching Heart

The sweet pain of the Aching Heart
Is a solace to the soul, you should know...

You teased me and tricked me into loving you
It was a truthful lie, and I believed in you

You fooled me as a child and drove away
Never to return a glance that you cared

You fixed your eyes and kissed me twice
Held my hands and said goodbye

My eyes disclosed the love, and you could know
The tears of love never did flow

Beloved my love for you is hard to show
And you are too far to touch and glow

I'll never let my lips talk of love
Only if you carried a Heart, you would know...

Especially For You...

Nay nay, and why why I keep muttering all day
You get irritated and I love to make you feel that
way

Chocolates and flowers I don't need any
anyways
Kisses and hugs are all, and I'll give you in
many ways

Does distance make our hearts grow fonder?
I would prefer to be close and not grow fonder...

People do wonder about you and me
Naming our relationship is so very tricky

Love and love is all I have for you
Sealed with kisses are my poems for you

Had I but one life to spend with you
Wonder I would only do things just for you...

Lost

Is this me? Roaming like a lost child
Begging for pardon that I never could find
Will my love ever be defined?
As I wait for the dusk in my life!

Promises and caring, I have them all
Are they true? I judge them not
Gems and stars I ask from none
Give me some hope is all I want...

Cheat me not – my feelings, please spare
Lonely I am, untouched flower that's rare
Dancing along the tunes of life astray
Believe in me, that's all I pray...

You have a world, and I am not a part
Urge you to know I crave to be gone
Wandering bee – I'll remain to be
Waiting not for a word from thee...

No one surrounds to hear my cry
Why I plead and tear my heart?
Trust and faith deceive my path
Lost I am longing to be found! ! !

Avid Feelings...

Tender love filled my senses
Longing thirst, in air it vanished
Hearts collided with a rhythm so right
Insistent desires filled a long-lost trial

Trailing fingers spurred up my soul
Sweet whispers told a tale untold
Gone are my scents and left me cold
Am struggling with my breath; behold

So amorous that special night was
The moon shied and hid in the skies above
Darkness crammed space, alight with kisses was
Holding us tight, love engulfed us both

Is all this love only for me?
Locked in your heart secure for me
Pouring on me with content filled
Or is there a doubt lurking therein?

Bliss and joy surround the creation
Songs of cuckoo I love and admire them, dear
Nostalgic feelings creep beneath my being
Smile rests on my face, as if this is all just a
dream...

Thine Alone!

Rain and Sunshine are not mine alone
Rainbows and Flowers are not mine alone
My love for Thee is mine alone
Ask for Peace and Blessing alone

Rest all things are dust alone
Desire for the unknown is better left alone
Suffering in my life is not mine alone
Tears in my heart are not mine alone

Lord with me, share these alone
I believe in Faith and Faith alone
Jesus is my Saviour is the Truth alone
Lord is always with me, and I am His alone...

Joys of Motherhood

Motherhood, a journey, both powerful and kind,
A tapestry woven with threads divine.
In the cradle of life, a sacred bond unfolded,
In love's pure essence, bonds were molded.

From the first flutter of life within,
To the moment I held you, my heart did spin.
With each heartbeat, a new chapter unfurled,
In your embrace of love, my soul found its
world.

In your eyes, I saw galaxies great,
A realm of love, blooming rare.
Your tiny fingers, a touch so divine,
In your innocence, pure love did shine.

With each step you took, my heart soared high,
Guiding you with love beneath the sky.
Through valleys low and mountains steep,
Together, we walked, our bond to keep.

In your dreams, I see tomorrow's glow,
An empty canvas with hopes to sow.
Through tears and triumphs, you'll find your way,
In the dance of growing up, day by day.

Now as you spread your wings to fly,
Know that in my heart, my blessings lie.
For in your journey, mine I see,
A tapestry of love, bound eternally.

So, here's to us, my precious children,
In the melody of life, forever acquiesced.
For in your eyes, my soul doth find,
The love of motherhood, as I'm defined.

GUL MOHAR

Royal Poinciana you call it or Flame Tree, as it
may
This Flamboyant tree, I'll cherish always as the
Gulmohar flame
The bursting of stunning hues of reds, yellows,
and oranges
Are a sight to behold every summer when these
blooms grace us

Leaves are as delicate as ferns, but the flower, it
flaunts and makes a statement
My heart lays captured and soul utterly lost as I
gaze at this beauty enchant
The colossal spread of this mighty tree brings
forth a veil of foliage luxuriant
Array of pictorial and aesthetic delight, the
gathered buds lay a quaint delight

Often my breath skips a turn as I marvel at this
God's most amazing work
Could there be any better showpiece on this
earth to complete His mastery
The flow of the branches with bundles of
blooms, a spectacle you can't miss
The fallen petals mask the ground and fashion
for me a red carpet greet

Love for Gul Mohar is an ethereal reality for you
and me
We both fell in love with this ineffable sight of
the tree
It has incarcerated and imprinted our secrets for
ages to come
This tree will always remind me of the day when
we lay bare and pure

My love for this magnificent display of a
marvelous and stunning tree,
encompasses beyond the words of a literary
view and understanding.
My wish is that when the days are gone, lay me
underneath a Gulmohar tree
Or plant a sapling where I lie, and my soul shall
bloom every summer that passes by.

The Spring

The mighty king with its wing
Is knocking at my door...

The night's gone, the sun's dawn
The sleeping flowers rise...

The rainbow fades, the birds awake
The wind is passing by...

The color's bloom, the plants sprout
The spring is coming by...

Entwined beyond yonder

Entwined are we from eternities and eons gone
by...

The war of the hearts is how it all began,
With shyness of the eyes caught between our
glances
In your presence, the poor pulses are racing
Melting my limbs in the lovingness of your
glimpses

Compelling and fierce is our bond in which we
reveal
Sneaking and pilfering every precious moment
in real
From the snarling and glaring gazes that
surround
Untouched and blithe, our love breathes, though
apart!

The fate of my life is decided and decreed
To spend the days on this foxhole and beyond
with thee
As lovers we remain, mates and partners never
Soul to soul we shall meet in every life, here's a
promise to thee…

Darker than dark

Darker than dark is a phrase I have often used
Portrays my soul with deep secrets taken roots
Just like a shadow, these have been ingrained
within
These would stain everything if it sees the light
therein

Darkness of thoughts brings a plethora of
queries
Should you ever leave, the world would cease to
be
Darkness of the night doesn't compare to the
emptiness of my feelings
The passions of your love, my darling, could
shatter the glass ceiling.

Many a thing that a darker than dark could be
Not the love that hit rock bottom and lay in the
depths of the sea.
It took all my strength, vigor, and many
lifespans to return and be
If ever the darkness engulfs, do not seek, as I
would have buried me

I believe in light, but darkness rules in the
absence of the day
Not just me, even the moon that I speak to
during twilight says,
Dark is the pathway packed with beastly
creatures all along the way
I plead for the light that you readily give, it will
break the darkness away…

Shooting Star

To wish upon a shooting star, I really wish I
could
Couple of wishes that are locked away in my
heart
Are bubbling away to be let out and loose

Falling star for few, a desire granting knave for
others
For me, you are a Star, a star that I have lost my
everything to
To wish upon you or you are my wish, am
figuring out that too

The star that falls wants to know and is asking
me,
Would you catch me if I fell out of the sky?
Every time, will I hold you, and yet again, I will!

You are my wishes come true and not a dream
The desires of my being are inscribed in your
being
Pride I will not let come to me, vanity, I forego

Star-cross lovers we may be, but lovers we are
Everyone longs to fulfill their wishes upon you

I simply yearn to become your want and desire
too

Let not fear cross your heart, we are destined to
be
The stories, when told, of besotted love in the
galaxies
You and I are to be engraved and reminisced
ceaselessly...

Thank I thee

A drop in the universe, I see myself reeling
Extraneous and superfluous in the blueprint of living
How would I matter if ever I cease to exist
It's just a matter of time and the direction of the wind
and I would be blown away in a flash into non-being.
But today I matter, I do, and I know for sure
coz I am placed in the midst of bonds that are pure
Most loving are my mother, father, and siblings dear
and affectionate my kins, extended families I treasure
Thank I thee, besides, to each and every friend I see
Being a part of my journey that wasn't that easy to be
This drop met an ocean that embraced every flaw in me
While submerged, I emerged a stronger myself in thee
Forgive my transgressions, for I remain arduous in eternity.

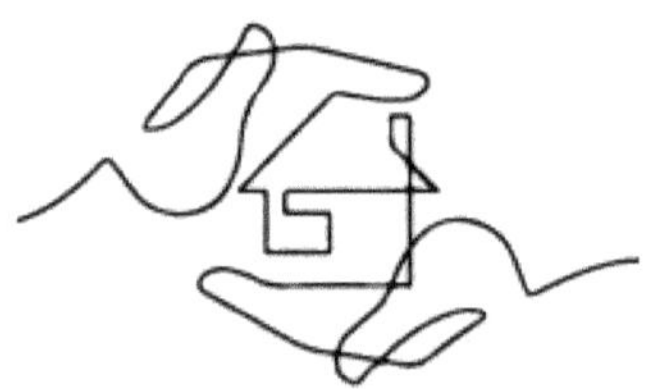

Eternally grateful

Visiting me often is a face familiar
Bringing forth the raptures that are unfamiliar.
Treasures hidden in the wave's anew
Finding my hope in the tracks you drew.

I am burying that pain, and now what remains
Tucked away somewhere are those gems.
Fiddling your way are my imaginations
Marching away are my indignations.

In your arms today and then tomorrow not
My journey sails as a ship lacking a knot.
Holding my dreams, I sail along
Trusting my faith to set me aground.

It is you; I am sure who has me all shielded,
You were and remain my lifeline to this date
Alive I am with the touch of your hands and
tender lips,
Eternally grateful, your existence hath bought
this bliss.

Jiji

(sister)

My Jiji... my lovely Jiji

God made thee for me
Someone who'd care and stand by me
Despite the trials, see me through with great
delight
You are the luck that people cross their fingers
twice
Blessed I am to be bestowed with your love and
grace divine

My Jiji… my lovely Jiji...

A sister so bold and beautiful with a heart of
gold
The watchful eyes, the caring smiles
Are the warmest along many miles
The inspiring words, the thoughtful deeds
Are the things others are deprived of

Sail Sail O' Cloud Mysterious

Sail Sail O' cloud mysterious
Sail home and nowhere else
Sail to me and give me rains...

Cover the earth with your wings
From the sun, please give us peace
The black beauty is my favorite
The silver lining is so very charming

The mighty thunder scares me a little
The crackling light makes me giggle
The earthly scents take me far
The chirping birds praise the Lord

Sail Sail O' cloud mysterious
Sail home and nowhere else
Sail to me and give me rains.

Friend

In the valley of dark, I found a light
With sweet smiles and twinkling eyes
The words were warm
The souls were drawn
The thoughts that drove the grief afar

In time, you became my friend, most dear
With constant care and cheerful laughs
Holding your arm, I walked along
You, my friend, I will cherish for Life...

Spectacular Twilights

Have you ever seen the sky explode?

On a lovely summer evening, the sun is ready to
set out,
When the blue is at its supreme contrast at large,
The perkiest shades of oranges are magical and
bright.
Just take in the beauty of this sparsely clouded
sky,
For this is when the sky is preparing for a show
of the twilight.

The sunset will be gone just as quickly as it
appears,
It teaches you to embrace each and every
moment as they come.
Sunsets are to die for, and doesn't matter where
you see them from;
Surely, it's easy to adore it on the beach with the
palm trees on the sides,
But do take out time and enjoy, as it's equally
captivating underneath the urban lights.

The sun is an artist and a very popular one at
that too
It has inspired diverse talents like many famous
artists do
Lot has been written on sunrise and its profound
impact on human lives
Sunsets are looked upon as a winding-down
scene from books or movie files...
When I see these radiantly bright skies, I am
reminded of the bitter but distinct truth

That the endings can be beautiful too...

BOOZO

(pet)

You are precious and precious of all
I will never have another to replace your bark

Your looks are like none other
The sidewalk is yours, and that's how you move

Boozo is your name, and you seem to know
You trail every path and always keep a faithful
watch

You sleep in my bed and share my pillow
You guard my room and patiently wait for me.

Nuts and chocolates are your favorite
But you don't eat a meal unless gently fed
Kids are elated, and adults admire
Elegantly when you walk and jump on their
stride

You get away with many of your wicked ways
Everyone loves to hate you,
and I only & only love you...

The smile

Standing in the midst of flowers
Thinking with the depth of wonder
Flows through air the unsaid phrases
There the solitude surrounding her graces

Will she speak, will she sing
Thousands of voices reach my ear
Mysterious smile covers her face
The birds are starring, flowers are still

The blinking eyes, the trembling lips
Searching for a heart to leap
She holds the beauty of a twilight eve
Blurring the night with sadness filled
Was the smile a mystery or a dream...

Wedding Grace

Two souls meet, and they forever unite
Thoughtful words and prayers combine

Showers of Love all around spread
Diverse, but together, two families embrace

The time is ripe, and we all arise
To celebrate this wedding – a promise sublime

Let us give thanks to God so great
For He bestows this hour – a blessed grace...

Essence of an essence

What am I, if not the blood that runs in your
veins
What I am, if not the light in your deepest grave
Perhaps I am the song that you try hard to
remember
Or just the breath that holds you together

Lover's light I am, the warmth of a winter night
The sun that shines despite the clouded skies
I am the needle to the thread, seaming through
life
Or just the plain sight and promise of the
rainbow arc

Let me be the words of your mouth when you
speak
Let me be the vision of what you want to see
Merely let me be a shadow when you step out in
the sun
Or just the scent on your clothes that you carry
along

Willfully and patiently, I wait for a place in your
heart
Marking my steps on the roads that you have
passed
You are more than the map, you know all
directions
Be my compass and lead, to meet my journey's
dissolution.

Lovers' Quandary

The craving for a beloved is greater than any
measure
If there's one who denies they are telling a
soulful lie
Lovers' presence in plain sight or far far away
Will always tug your heart in so many many
ways

The touch of a lover, or just a trailing finger
A passing remark or a brush of the shoulder
The gentle smile with a smirk in lovers' eyes
Leaves us wanting more, a wild desire

Years have passed and the craving's still on
The youthful flame or the gilded withering age
Sometimes hidden, other times openly gazed
Tells you many stories of lovers wanting craze

Wish we could be tied down, but that's a
dreadful ask
You and I are lovers who are locked in this
blissful rut
Isolate us, and we'll rot and remain in that rueful
mut
Together we are and remain privileged as lovers
must.

Betrayal

Love brings us to so many turns,
We lose sight of looming returns
Carried away by the heart's foolish ways
Seemingly smartness takes flight and deserts
away

Why do my senses seem thus fleeting?
Though I live with perceptible deceits therein
I have perpetually been patient and kind
Trusting and believing you are forevermore
mine

Betrayed by your words that sought sympathy
You are clever and smart, and I gave myself
completely
Simply a foolish lover, spent a lifetime lingering
Hopeful that someday you will discern the
misgivings

Missteps I forgive, not the deed of your betrayal
Suspicions cloud the mind and pierce the heart
fatal
Would you have ever reached out and made the
mend
These are still my worries that need a truthful
end.

Own me

Gentle are your words, pleasant your manners
Caring your nature, mellifluous your songs
Brimming with love, an aura your life expels
You build bridges and make people dwell

Fortunate my life that you are a part of it
Thank Lord for Every single day and night
Glows my heart at the thought of being alive
In the knowledge, your love is eternally mine

The look in your eyes tells me that;
If I were a diamond, you would flaunt me
If I were a sweet, you would devour me
If I were a road, you would travel on me

The touch of your hands means that;
If I ever fall, you will be there to catch me
If I need a shoulder, your arms will hold me
If I am afraid, you will be around to protect me

These feelings, my love, overflow my desires
To be in your company, and only to be loved
Singularly I would give anything to be your
fame
Unabashedly own me, that would be my gain…

Goodbyes

Farewells do bring heartache, and lovers know it
well
Suffered it when you picked your cases and
opened the gates
My soul shivered when your lips touched mine
for that brief second
That moment, my heart felt an emptiness that I
never knew existed

I said a "Goodbye," coz an eternity passes every
time we're apart
Being away from you is a hard-hitting reality
and an arduous combat
Every second is rough, not just those months
when we await our date
Even a trifling goodnight rips and tears my soul
away

Separation brings a tryst with self that I cannot
explain
When will this anguish vanish and these partings
only a custom
Pray we are together always, walking hand in
hand, and I your shadow remain
Hope these goodbyes stop to matter and my eyes
smile despite your absence.

In the arms of death

There is a fear that surrounds us incessant,
the dread of the unknown heavens revealing
More than the aftermath at the end of our lives,
the thoughts of losing your triumphs in this life.
Nothing holds me down so dear on this earth
the dullness of the mud cannot compare to the
riches stored in the Lord's house
When the time is up and I will gladly say
Goodbye
the fleeting spell will be left behind.
My soul galore with praise and spirit rejoicing
In the arms of death, I'll find my peace yearning
free from the clinches and snares alighting.
The promised land will I find and relishing,
is the sole comfort when death will come
knocking…

Escapade

Funny if I would call our love story by any other
name
Frolicking our way into making our own
fairytale
Life has been anything but kind to us
Pocketing these moments is the only resolution

Sneaking and creeping like young lovers do
Seizing every occasion with zeal and fervor to
Like a hungry lion eyeing its prey
We live by and wait for that perfect plan to
frame…

We've found our joy in the tiny spheres of life
Life was drifting without a purpose, a river
flowing
Hanging in there, delicate balance swinging
We continue to rendezvous and keep our love
floating

These escapades have become a part of me
I would fade into the realms if they stop you and
me
My true self surfaces, and I emerge visible with
you
For sweeping me away on these voyages, my
heart bellows a big thank you

When we unite

I often sit back and think
what will life be like when we unite
The gush of the passions and urges of our hearts
will be visible from miles away

We will bond like honey and milk
dwell in our tiny abode like a love nest built.
The charred fate that buried our love for years
will surface swiftly and bring heaps of cheers

Gladiolus with dew drops on its lips
hold thee I will, with honor and revere
My silence and my tears will reveal a story
untold,
jitters will fade, concealing all those years

Separation caused a grief untold and unheard
Heart let out a beat that was cold and unnerved
The rain did drench me lacking any hesitation
The sigh I felt was unmistakably filled with
trepidation

Nonetheless, I still hope we will win
With battered grief and pain within.
Why did I hide my feelings so potent and
strong?
If I didn't, you should have carried the baton
along

Life is long and with kindness filled
There will be many destinations and we'll strive
to meet
Keep our love strong for both of us, fail if I
may!
We'll allow the passions to guide us, please as
they may!

Beautiful Encounter....

I feel complete!
Strange as it may sound
Calmness, my heart finally found
Restless were the thoughts that now stay still
In the warmth of your arms, I feel complete!

Love divine!
It heals my heart and gladdens thy soul
It petrifies my past; thus, it lies buried in a grave
unknown
Sings a song that stirs my nerves and softens my
pain
Engulfed in the embrace, I trust and believe, in
love divine!

Forever is true!
These words never meant a thing
Till you came along bearing a ring
Forgive me, my darling, now my doubts
unfound remain
Believing and trusting your presence foretold,
now forever is true!

Beautiful Encounter!
Met an acquaintance incomparable
Kissed the lips, dipped in wine and unforgettable
The violent gush of pleasures engulfed me, in
the waves of adoration
Willfully I surrendered, to the peace of this
Beautiful Encounter!